MW01050094

Timeshare Owners

Don't get Scammed!

www.timeshare-scams.org

Disclaimer of Liability and Warranties

General Disclaimer and Limitation of Liability:

To order additional copies, please contact us.
BookSurge
www.booksurge.com
1-866-308-6235
orders@booksurge.com

Exposed: The latest Timeshare Scams that are deceiving thousands of unsuspecting Timeshare Owners world-wide.

Table of Contents

Just in case anyone is very dubious about the information provided in this book, we would like to add that we have no personal connection or financial interest in any Timeshare companies; hence no companies are listed or promoted. There is also no advertising or product placement in this book.

The Timeshare Scams that are in operation world-wide are changing all the time. By the time you read this book, there will be several new editions to the scams listed here. That is why we publish a companion site and email newsletter for this book.

www.timeshare-scams.org

Here you will find Timeshare Scam updates plus comments from fellow Timeshare owners.

If you have questions about this book or anything else related to Timeshare Scams please write to us at

info@timeshare-scams.org

We look forward to hearing from you.

The Timeshare-Scams Team,

WHY THIS BOOK?

To you, the reader and Timeshare Owner please do not expect this book to be of the same reading quality as a New York Times Bestseller! But do expect this book to provide you and the six million plus Timeshare Owners worldwide, with priceless information that could help prevent you from losing money in the future.

The people at Timeshare-scams.org are not professional authors. This book is not meant to have the writing excellence of a best seller that will win a major book prize. It is written as we speak, and we ask you to read this as if we are speaking to you direct, face to face. We would like to get a message across that will warn Timeshare Owners, and give details of evidence that we have found about Timeshare Scams, as well as provide helpful tips on the selling or renting of your Timeshare. Our mission is to be a trusted advisor when it comes to information on Timeshare.

The internet is filled with websites and individuals that claim to have the inside know how and experience on how to sell your Timeshare. With so much information available it is very hard to find who to trust.

Sold the right way, Timeshare is an amazing product that can provide many families great value in taking vacations. Yet you cannot hide from the fact that it can be a very hard product for an owner to sell.

We also know that by exposing these fraudulent ways of deceiving Timeshare Owners, many of these companies that are active in these scams will accuse us on forums, and book review sites, saying how we are only trying to put a bad name on the Timeshare Business.

All we ask is that you, the reader, be the judge of the material that you read in this book. It is a simple message to put across and warn unsuspected Timeshare Owners of potential scams that are happening in the world today, and share some tips on how to rent or sell your Timeshare. We praise all the Resale companies that successfully sell or rent Timeshare for owners and wish them success. Of course any companies that operate in a professional ethical way would have no problems with this book and we hope that they will support it and help market our book to their data base of clients. This book is to help and support the Timeshare industry. An industry, that in 2005 provided $92 billion to the US economy.

What's in it for us? We receive a small royalty from the sale of each book, we say small as we have priced this book as low as we can, in order for as many people to see the book for the real value it holds, and to hope it gets to as many Timeshare Owners as possible.

It is our idea that details of these Scams ought to be placed within reach of Timeshare Owners, who do

not have time to investigate how Timeshare Owners are scammed.

When you approach a book with a subject like this, you could be entering very suspicious untrustworthy territory. To some, it may seem that we are making accusations at certain companies that we believe operate in an unethical way of doing business. To others, it may look like we are discontented Timeshare Owners who have been scammed and feel like this is the only way to fight back.

It may also appear that we are angry ex employees who have been dismissed from our jobs and still have not been paid any outstanding commissions. By writing a book like this we can bring shame to these companies and hope it affects their business.

We have looked at many options in which to put our message across, so as not to name any individuals or companies. One idea we had was to write this book as a fictional story about a John and Mary who bought a Timeshare and follow their lives for a year going into great detail about what happened. Unfortunately John lost his job, his finances started to dry up and Mary too was not working at that time so they felt the best thing to do was to try and sell their Timeshare. In doing this, they entered the world of Timeshare Resale's. They dealt with the wrong company and the end result was that they were duped out of a lot of money and still owned their Timeshare.

They also had friends who were very happy with their Timeshare, but suffered a constant bombardment of phone calls every night and were promised that there were buyers who would offer double what they had originally paid for their Timeshare! All they had to do was just pay an upfront fee to register which would be fully refundable if the sale fell through. This they found very hard to resist as it was such a tempting offer. But regrettably it never happened and they too lost money. This though could end up sounding like a soap story and would it be believable? Plus it would just be writing a bad view on Timeshare Ownership which may put potential buyers off in the future.

We know that Timeshare is an amazing product and brings great vacations to over six million Timeshare Owners every year.

We also know that The Timeshare business, like any other business, has good and bad companies, so please note that this book has not been written to just put a bad view on Timeshare Companies. We are sure for certain, that there are many companies in the Timeshare world today that operate in an honest, trustworthy and ethical way of doing business.

AND you must understand that if a Timeshare Owner chooses to pay a fee to advertise their Timeshare through a company that will market their week and place advertisements for them on a web site and deal with all enquires, then that is the choice of the Timeshare Owner and where is the bad practice in that?

We think everyone would agree though, that it is very bad practice to promise someone that there is a buyer for their Timeshare, take funds from the seller, assuring them that this is to assist in the sale going through, yet when the sale does not materialize, refuse to refund the money. Well is that fair? Questions need to be asked, was there ever a buyer? Or is this a complete scam?

Is it fair to send innocent Timeshare Owners a false check, made payable in their names, for a very large amount of money backed up with a professional looking letter stating that their Timeshare has been sold? In order for the funds to be released, so the check will clear, all they have to do is pay the tax due on this amount. Of course, this is done only for the check to bounce and the Timeshare is still not sold. Is this a good way of promoting a Timeshare business?

Is it fair to be offered your Timeshare in part exchange for another one, only six months later the part exchange does not happen and you end up owning both and now having to pay two amounts of annual fees?

Worldwide there are many different ways of advertising your goods for sale and these all cost varying amounts of money. A front page advert in a main publication, of course will cost more than a small three line add in a local free news paper. It is down to the Timeshare Owner how they choose to advertise their Timeshare for sale, if they wish to sell it. Though what we see happening is that 99.9% of all owners who decide to sell their Timeshare have no experience in the industry, so of course the best route is to take advice from companies that operate in the Timeshare business.

Naturally, like any consultancy company, it is right if you go to someone for advice or assistance, they will charge you a fee, and this is how businesses operate. Unfortunately, there are some companies that play on the fact that you want to sell your Timeshare and as you have no experience on how to do it, they will charge you ridiculously large amounts of money under false promises. We would like to share with you advice and warn you of the many false and misleading bad practices that are in operation today.

This book will share tips on selling your Timeshare where you can advertise for free, yes **FREE!** Even if you wish to pay a company to sell your Timeshare, of course look at the options where you place free ads, this will only give you more exposure. Timeshare-scams.org will also share good tips on the content of your advert, who to target and why we believe you should consider renting out your Timeshare as well.

We also list the most current Timeshare Scams that are occurring around the world today and have happened to thousands of innocent Timeshare Owners. These are Scams! They are misleading ways to get money from you under false promises.

THEY ARE NOT A GIBE AT TIMESHARE RESALE COMPANIES THAT OFFER TO SELL YOUR TIMESHARE

FOR A FEE. As we have stated before, that is a way you can list your Timeshare for sale, if you choose.

THESE SCAMS NEED TO BE MADE KNOWN TO THE PUBLIC, AS INFORMATION FOR ANY TIMESHARE OWNER THAT WISHES TO SELL THEIR TIMESHARE, AND ADVICE TO THE INNOCENT OWNERS THAT HAVE NO WISH TO SELL, BUT ARE SUCKED INTO THE SLEEZY WORLD OF FALSE PROMISES AND LARGE CASH RETURNS THAT NEVER EXIST!

Have you ever been contacted by an unknown company and been told they have a buyer for your Timeshare? You probably have, and are not alone. Like the thousands of Timeshare Owners who have fallen prey to this and paid out money, only to find that their Timeshare remained unsold, you do not wish to talk about it! If this has not happened to you yet, and you own a Timeshare, then this book could stop you from losing thousands in the future.

Timeshare-scams.org does not sell Timeshare. We have a free e-mail subscription service, with website, to update you on the latest scams that we find in operation. The original intention of Timeshare-scams.org was to provide a website where you can advertise your Timeshare for sale or rent, at no cost. This though would be just another website along with the thousands of others that list Timeshares for sale. We will share with you in this book that advertising, along with the thousands of other Timeshares for sale does not always make great sense, and it may prove well to target a smaller market to help your listing stand out.

8

As we have mentioned before, this book is to be used as a guide, with as much "up to date" information on Timeshare Scams that we can provide at the time of going to print, and also provide you with tips on how to sell or rent your Timeshare.

Most owners who are trying to sell their Timeshare are unaware that their personal details are available to purchase. (It's no strange coincidence when you get that call!). They may have filled in a survey somewhere, or even been on a presentation and then had their details sold off to a marketing company. During our research writing this book, we have found that for only a few thousand dollars, we could purchase a list of over a million "Timeshare Owners" phone numbers and addresses, with full information on what they owned and when they bought.

"Good evening, we are so pleased to catch you at home! We understand you own a 2bed high season week at Palm Trees Beach Tennis Golf Ocean Resort. This resort is in such high demand; we have a list of buyers who are willing to pay double what you ask!"

"Your week is in such high demand, it will sell within days!"

"We have clients in Asia and Russia who want to buy into Timeshare. Only last week we sold the exact same Timeshare you own for $18,000. To be given the opportunity of being able to have an ownership certificate, they are willing to pay high prices for your week!"

These are just some of the thousands of lines that are used to entice a Timeshare Owner into handing over money, on a promise of more in return. It is very easy to trigger the "greed" emotion, and many times the conversation in the home is……

"Honey, they say we can get $20,000 for our week! The cash will be in our bank within 7 days……That's double what we paid; all we have to do is pay $500 registration fee. What do you think? It's a no brainer, we have nothing to lose!!"

The credit card details are given, and once more an unlucky couple has been tricked out of money.

What we have found is that after this has happened, clients feel embarrassed, and rather than fight the case and ask for their money back, they tend to stay quiet and put it down to experience. When you have thousands of people doing that every month the "Timeshare Scam" business runs into millions of dollars every year.

Over the following pages, we will list the top scams used by companies, plus other misleading tricks that you can expect.

TIMESHARE SCAMS

Scam: meaning…A fraudulent business scheme, a swindle, to defraud, deprive of by deceit,

At present the number of Timeshare Owners who wish to sell has increased dramatically. This is mainly due to the present world-wide economic circumstances and financial crisis. **Now more than ever, unsuspecting Timeshare Owners will be targeted and fall prey to the many Timeshare Scams in operation.** We repeat our message that it is our idea that these scams ought to be placed within reach of Timeshare Owners who do not have time to investigate how owners and potential Timeshare Owners are scammed.

The information that you will read over the next few pages will be quite shocking. You may think that it will be almost unbelievable and impossible that anyone could fall victim to these fraudulent ways of doing business. Those that read this, and have been targeted before, will feel comfort that they are not alone when it comes to being pressured to part with money on the promise of their Timeshare being sold or rented at a substantiality high profit.

We share with you here just some of the Scams that have, and are still being used, to swindle Timeshare Owners and make them part with money under false promises.

PLEASE NOTE: WE DO NOT MENTION OR DIS- CRIMINATE ANY TIMESHARE RESALE OR RENTAL COM- PANIES. THE INFORMATION WE PROVIDE IS ONLY TO WARN AND ADVISE TIMESHARE OWNERS OF POTEN- TIAL SCAMS.

THIS INFORMATION CAN ONLY IMPROVE THE BUSINESS FOR ALL TIMESHARE COMPANIES THAT SELL OR RENT TIMESHARE IN A CORRECT, PROFESSIONAL, TRUSTWORTHY AND CREDIBLE WAY.

WE ARE KEEN TO POINT OUT THAT WE UNDER- STAND THAT THERE ARE TIMESHARES BEING SOLD AND RENTED EVERYDAY ALL AROUND THE WORLD. WE WOULD LIKE TO ADVISE AND PROTECT TIMESHARE OWNERS AND LET THEM MAKE THEIR OWN DECISIONS WHEN IT COMES TO SELLING OR RENTING THEIR TIME- SHARE. OUR MAIN ADVICE IS, IF IT SOUNDS TOO GOOD TO BE TRUE, IT PROBABLY IS, AND MANY TIMESHARE FORUMS WHICH GENUINE TIMESHARE OWNERS COM- MENT ON, WILL REINFORCE THIS STATEMENT.

Though that is a warning, please remember that there are professional sales people who are fully trained with very skilled and persuasive words that make the whole story sound completely different. In this book we have listed just some of the most popular scams that we know, there are of course many, many more. This list is changing all the time so please visit our website www.timeshare-scams.org for updates of any new scams that surface in the Timeshare World.

Unfortunately there are people that like to prey on the fact that you want to sell your Timeshare. They know that you "want out" for whatever reason and that you will be very happy to get your cash back as quickly as possible. This gives them the opportunity to make false promises, which thousands of Timeshare Owners fall for every year. The number one fact is, **if anyone demands a large amount of money upfront in return for selling or renting your Timeshare you must be very careful!** Why? Well in most situations when it comes to selling a product, isn't it normal practice to pay your commission once the product has been sold, not in advance?

There are also scammers that target Timeshare Owners who are very happy with their ownership and do not wish to sell. These scammers know that by making ridiculous offers and valuing their Timeshare at amounts double, sometimes even triple more than what they paid when they originally bought and then also claiming that there are buyers waiting to buy right now. Well these Timeshare Owners who never once thought of selling now find it hard to resist such an offer and are persuaded to sell. Another innocent couple again are drawn into the seedy world of Timeshare Scams.

If you are approached with an offer that may sound too good to be true, or even if you are just skeptical, before you part with any money do as much research as you can. You can e-mail timeshare-scams.org for free advice on **help@timeshare-scams.org** and we would also recommend that you search the web for Timeshare forums where you can post questions to other Timeshare Owners. This way you can get independent advice on the strength of what is being offered to you. It is known that many of the scammers pose as owners on forums. Thankfully though there are moderators that are wise to this. There are many Timeshare Forums that you can visit and all come with thousands of independent opinions on what is good and bad about Timeshare. Just type Timeshare Forums into any web search engine and you will find many of the top internet sites.

Your first concern should be that many Timeshare Owners personal details about what they own, and how to contact them, are available to buy. This is an unfortunate circumstance, yet as we have mentioned it is possible to purchase lists of hundreds of thousands of Timeshare Owners from marketing companies. There is no bad practice in that as these lists are sold in all sorts of forms as a way that companies can market their products to certain sectors of consumers. These lists are supposed to be used for selling or marketing products in a professional ethical way, not as a fraudulent business scheme.

You may have filled you personal details out while staying at a Timeshare resort, or even completed a survey when entering a prize draw to win a free vacation. The simple fact is that all Timeshare Owners at some point have attended a presentation, some more than once, and from that point onwards your information may be collected and can be passed on to companies that manage and sell data. So, if out of the blue you receive a call regarding the Timeshare you own, don't be too shocked, but this should be your first red flag. Why are they contacting me? Why am I the fortunate person? It has also been known that some of the companies that operate these scams just take pot luck and cold call from a telephone book asking if you own a Timeshare.

We now list the most current Scams that are at present active in the Timeshare World Today.

Again visit **www.timeshare-scams.org** for information on any Timeshare Scams that surface.

Please note that most of these Scams will be presented to you via a phone call. This is the most productive way for these Scammers to sell their pitch. Of course with a letter that you receive in the post, you can always throw it away. Still, very recently with the new Do Not Call fines operating across the United States and the facility to now block incoming calls from certain numbers, a new postcard Scam is in operation. There are hundreds of thousands of post cards being sent around the world daily to Timeshare Owners and all it takes is a very small percentage to fall for the Scam to make this method profitable.

If not by phone call or post, to keep up with the latest technology, e-mail has now come into the fold, as thousands of e-mails can be sent just by one click. It is very easy to obtain e-mail addresses of Timeshare Owners, so be alert! It is also known that these Scams

can be presented to you at a presentation. This can make them even more believable, as you are having face to face contact which, like when you bought your Timeshare, can be more convincing!

Scam 1

To start with, we list one of the most popular scams, which is where you will receive a phone call from a company to say that they have a buyer for your Timeshare.

Think about this, someone you have never heard of before, decides to give you a phone call with the unbelievable information that **THEY** have a client who wants to buy your Timeshare. This is amazing, and at first you would be quite shocked, but it's true, you have been desperate to sell and now you have been told that someone wants to buy and at the price you are asking.

"Good evening, is that Mr. Johnson? I understand you are selling your Timeshare at xxxxx resort. Well, I have some very good news; we have a client who wants to buy your week".

If this was REALLY TRUE, then why would they not buy the Timeshare from you and then re-sell it to the potential purchaser at a higher price? Still, this is a fact; thousands of Timeshare Owners every year get a phone call to say there is someone who wants to buy their Timeshare.

You, the Timeshare Owner, of course get excited as you have been trying to sell your Timeshare for months, sometimes even years. So where is the SCAM?

Before it sounds too good to be true you will be asked for a "refundable" deposit. You will be told that you have to pay this to ensure that you go through with the transaction.

"Yes Mr. Johnson that is correct our clients are willing to pay the $15,000 you are asking, we have spent a lot of time in communication with them as they have been looking at many different resorts in the area where you own. To complete the transaction we ask for a refundable deposit of $500. This is to guarantee that the transaction goes through from your end and I repeat, if the sale falls through of course this fee is fully refundable."

First off, why would anyone have to pay a deposit to make sure that they let someone buy their Timeshare????? How many houses or cars….in fact what products do you know of that to be sold, the seller pays a deposit, to make sure they let the sale go through!!!!

Please remember, you will be speaking to a Sales Professional who is trained in this department, has a lot of skill and talent in making everything sound all ok and trustworthy. Most of the time their background is from selling Timeshare's before.

What happens though is that you end up paying the deposit. This deposit can range from $200 to $2,000, sometimes even higher. It's not your fault, but you fall for the smooth talking and because you have been waiting so long to sell your Timeshare and now you finally get a bit of action, this may seem like a risk worth taking. You feel it is going to happen and you don't want to lose the buyer.

Another reason most people pay, is that they are told that the deposit is only taken if you fail to complete the transaction. So with all these safety guarantees you give your credit card number, yet the money is still taken anyway.

A week or two goes by and the buyer fails to complete. Why? Because there probably was never a buyer in the first place! And your deposit will thereafter be referred to as a 'fee.'

This is where the scam really takes off.

You now get another call, all apologetic; to say that they are so sorry the deal fell through.

"Hi Mr. Johnson, unfortunately there has been a problem with the sale of your Timeshare, and the buyer is having difficulties with his funds. It was so close, they really wanted it but they have had trouble with finance their end. Still, don't worry, we have placed your resort on our premium listing and we have already had a few enquires so expect it to sell soon".

"But what about my refundable deposit?"

"Don't worry about it Mr. Johnson, as promised this will be fully refunded. We will now actually continue to sell your Timeshare for you, for free! Our company gets over a thousand enquires a week from potential buyers and we have now put your week on our star buys section, and if we cannot find someone to buy your Timeshare within the next 6 months, the whole fee will be refunded."

This is just an example of the sort of script that you will be pitched. It will vary in many ways, and be adapted to fit the situation and will be backed up again with a lot of convincing, smooth talking promises, of how they have the right clients and you will sell your Timeshare as it is in high demand. To add to the pressure on you and how they completely turn the situation round a line that often works is......!

"If we do not act on your behalf Mr. Johnson your Timeshare is just going to sit there, it will not sell itself will it? You can trust us, this is our business, and we have sold millions of dollars of Timeshare, check our website and read our Testimonials."

Most of the time, as this is your first experience in this situation, you feel quite good, as after nothing happening there still seems to be a lot of activity regarding the selling of your Timeshare. You have no experience in selling Timeshare and they are right, if you do nothing it is not going to sell itself.

Six months later though and at much disappointment to you no progress has been made. To make this scam even more unreal, unbeknown to you, your details are then sold to another Timeshare company who contact you and offer to buy your Timeshare. Wow!! This is great news, all you have to do is go and visit them. You will then be invited to their company headquarters, and of course please don't forget your proof of ownership certificates, and make sure all your fees are paid up to date.

This presentation will most likely be a with a specialist company that claim to buy back Timeshares. Your visit to them really is a Timeshare presentation, where they will offer to buy your Timeshare, ONLY in a part exchange if you buy theirs!!! You of course refuse and leave after a few hours of hard sell and lots of promises.

After all this, you then get a call from the original company that started this whole process. They contact you to tell you they will not refund you the fee they charged because they found a buyer for you. ***"It's not their fault that you turned the offer down."***

Now six months on and you are still trying to sell your Timeshare and you are a huge fee out of pocket.

All this started from a phone call from someone offering to buy your Timeshare!

Scam 2

Another Scam, which is pretty simple, is where money will be deducted from your credit card or bank account after you receive a pitch from a company that claims they will sell or rent your Timeshare. This scam does not just target owners wishing to sell their Timeshare. This targets all six million plus Timeshare Owners.

With this call, the introduction will most likely be... ***"We understand that you own a Timeshare. Do you want to rent it or sell it? We offer a FREE service for Timeshare Owners".***

In most cases you would refuse, as like most Timeshare Owners you are happy, and using your ownership. But the call will continue with mind dazzling offers of the company claiming to be renting your week for thousands of dollars, and do not have enough weeks to meet the demand, or the fact that the exact week that you own sold for an incredibly high price only last week. (This will most likely be double what you paid, when you bought your Timeshare.)

The caller will claim to be a "Professional Timeshare Company", with years of experience, and that they are also members of approved Timeshare organizations. This will be backed up with a website including numerous testimonials from all their happy customers.

Once again through no fault of your own, as many people fall for the smooth talking words, you find what is offered very irresistible, who wouldn't? **For FREE, a com-**

**pany is offering to rent or sell your Timeshare and pay
you once the transaction is done**.

You like what they have to offer so agree to what they
say; the only thing is they need your credit card details or
bank details so they can pay you when the transaction goes
through.

The shock to you is a few weeks later when you find
your card has been deducted a large amount of money, or
your bank calls you saying there is a transfer of funds await-
ing your approval. (At this time you may get a 2nd call saying they took the funds as they have a buyer, paper work
should all be completed in the next few weeks) Be very
careful here, as all this does is extend the time and make
sure that they have the funds from you. It is the Timeshare
Owners who are desperate to sell that fall for this more often, and the scammers can feel this, so it makes it easier
to, once again, **"fall for the pitch"**. The owners feel if they
turn down the offer, they may never get this opportunity
again. At this point many people again pay out money on
the promise their Timeshare will be sold and end up still
owning their Timeshare.

This is the Scam, money being deducted from your
credit-card or bank account for no reason. Your Timeshare
has not been sold or rented; this is not what was promised.

**AGAIN PLEASE NOTE...THERE ARE MANY PRO-
FESSIONAL COMPANIES, WORLDWIDE, THAT OFFER**

A SERVICE TO RENT OR SELL YOUR TIMESHARE AND ARE OPERATING AND DOING BUSINESS IN A CORRECT, PROFESSIONAL WAY. THE MAIN FACT IS THAT THEY DO NOT TAKE FUNDS FROM YOU WITHOUT REASON. THEY EITHER TELL YOU THEY CHARGE A FEE, FOR ACTING ON YOUR BEHALF TO SELL YOUR TIMESHARE, AND CAN NOT GUARANTEE IT WILL BE SOLD. OR, CHARGE ADVERTISING FEES TO LIST YOUR TIMESHARE ON THEIR WEBSITE. AGAIN, THEY WILL NOT GUARANTEE THAT YOUR TIMESHARE WILL BE SOLD AT ALL.

OUR WARNING IS TO THE SCAM OF BEING PROMISED A FREE SERVICE AND MONEY BEING TAKEN FROM YOU, WITHOUT ANY SELLING OR RENTING OF YOUR TIMESHARE.

Why would you have to give any credit card details or bank account numbers to a company offering to sell or rent your Timeshare for free? If the service is for free then no credit card numbers need to be given, as no funds need to be taken until any transaction is proven.

Scam 3

This follows on to a cold call you will receive. This is the same as Scam Two but a different script. This time though they will mention that **they do want an advance payment.** The advance payment is to pay for the marketing and advertising of your Timeshare. There really is nothing wrong with this apart from the ridiculously high fees that they charge. There are many of these advertising companies in operation. They charge an advertising fee to place your Timeshare as a listing on their website. It's just that there are some charging very high fees and charge different clients different amounts, all depending on how much they feel they can get off you.

This should be a practical way to sell your Timeshare, as in order for your Timeshare to get noticed above all the other tens of thousands of Timeshares worldwide this company pay for high premium advertising on TV, radio and all major newspapers and publications. Many also pay for internet advertising so that their site comes up high in the search engine rankings. Compared to a high street shop with Timeshares for sale listed in the window this actually can be one of the best ways to sell your Timeshare.

Good news you think, and this call will be backed up with a script of how they are not like other companies and that they really work for their clients. This is a very competitive market and you will not just get the one phone call, expect many!!!! Just be warned about the elevated fees that start at $500 and work up as high as $2,000 and more.

To be fair you should always pay for high profile advertisement so where is the scam?
The scam here is when you are promised that your Timeshare will sell within weeks, if not your whole funds will be returned. Notice that they call you and **PROMISE** that if you pay this high advertisement fee they guarantee that your Timeshare will be sold.

Many Timeshare Owners find 12 months down the road they still own their Timeshare, and getting the funds back that they were promised if it does not sell can prove to be very difficult and mostly impossible. At this stage with funds already paid, many of the different scams that are listed here come into play. A simple line you may hear is:

"We are sorry Mr. Johnson, due to the current market conditions, it seems that we have had a dip in our Timeshare Resales, but to compensate this we will list your Timeshare for free on our website until it sells. Completely free of charge Mr. Johnson. We are still getting thousands of hits to our website; it will only be a matter of time. Last month we sold over a million dollars of Timeshare."

That sounds fair enough, but really you have paid $1,000, or whatever fee you paid, to have your Timeshare listed on a website, along with thousands of others, and all selling at different prices, most probably lower than yours. Remember they promised you that your Timeshare would be sold, guaranteed, or you will receive a full refund.

We have spoken to many Timeshare Owners who say once they have advertised their Timeshare in this way they have had no inquires by phone or e-mail with offers to buy their Timeshare. In fact, once they paid this fee and advertised, they actually got more calls from many different companies claiming that they can do a better service and get them more for their Timeshare.

If you have paid a large sum to advertise your Timeshare, how many calls or offers have you received?

Simple fact is to do your research. There are many options where you can advertise for free or at least for a sensible amount of money, and we will share that with you later in this book.

Surely if this was the best way to sell Timeshare with proven results, the companies that do this could make more money if they took fees over and above what the Timeshare Owner wanted.

When speaking to owners who had been called and pitched the *"pay us $500 and we promise to sell your Timeshare for you"*....Call. The call often states that they promise to sell your Timeshare for thousands more than you paid.

"We know you purchased your Timeshare for $10,000, well we can sell it for $15,000 that is the current market value."

This of course will get the Timeshare Owner excited thinking that a huge profit can be made. So paying the advertising fee is a no brainer. Yet, if this was a guaranteed sale then the company itself could make more money from the vast profit it can make from the sale of the Timeshare.

The better option is to set a price that you wish to sell your Timeshare for, say $10,000 and let the company take any funds over and above the amount they receive.

"If you can get $12,000 for my week then you can keep the "$2,000"

This can be proven to good effect when you get the call saying your Timeshare is worth $20,000!!!!!! ***Just pay us $2,000 and we will sell it for you within the next 2 weeks.**"* Rather than pay the $2,000, explain to them that this is great news, "**rather than $2,000 I would be happy to pay you $10,000 as I only want $10,000 back on my Timeshare.**" In most cases they will promise to get back to you, but never call again. They have called a Timeshare Owner who has done their research.

Congratulations, you may have just saved yourself thousands of dollars.

Scam 4

This Scam is one of the most popular and the one that costs most innocent Timeshare Owners the most money. There are two pitches here. One will be where you get a call from a company saying that they have found someone who wants to rent your Timeshare. This could be a complete cold call from a company you have never heard of. But to make the scam work and become even more believable, they would have pre called you six months prior and offered to list Your Timeshare for Rental for FREE on their website. They will market for you and only take a commission once it has been rented.

28

"Good evening Mr. Johnson, we are calling from xxxxx Timeshare rentals. We only deal in high quality Timeshares that we list for rent on our website and through our world-wide marketing company. We are very successful at this and regularly rent Timeshares in the area that you own for $2,000 to $4,000 per week. We are experiencing a high demand of requests for apartments; condos and villa rentals this year and would like to list your week on our website. We ask for no upfront payment and do not require any bank or credit card details from you. Let us list your Timeshare and should we get an offer we will call you to see if you accept. Is that fair enough?"

This again is an example of the type of pitch you may receive; of course most times you will ask what is in it for them, for which the reply will be, they take a 20% commission. (This figure will vary). You will still stand to receive quite a hefty sum of money over and above your annual fees so when faced with an offer like this you have nothing to lose and all to gain.

So to recap here, this is a different version to Scam Three. This time they offer to rent your Timeshare for FREE, do not want any advance payment and do not want any of your credit card or bank details. They offer a free service, so of course you sign up.

Now a few months down the road you get the call saying that the company has been able to rent your week for you for $2,500. Please could you send them a $500 administration or commission fee.

NOW AT THIS POINT MOST PEOPLE WOULD ASK THEM TO DEDUCT THE FEE FROM THE MONIES THEY ARE DUE TO RECEIVE FROM RENTING.

Again this is where the scam, the real deception technique kicks in and a long list of reasons will be used which make sure you pay the fee first. It may sound totally unbelievable but it works. It is all about the timing and thought of that if the Timeshare Owners does not do it, they will lose the potential $2000.

"We would love to that Mr. Johnson, of course it would be much easier but this way saves YOU the rental tax that is due in Florida as we pay that for you from our end. If the transaction shows as 2 separate charges then you will have to pay."

"Mr. Johnson it is real estate law that all fees have to be paid in advance before we can confirm the transaction, this protects both of us. Remember as our contract states if the rental does not take place then all fess are fully refunded. If we do not take this fee now then we will offer the client an alternative option as they are very keen on going to Orlando."

They are a few examples of scripts that are used and they work. Thousands of Timeshare Owners on forums around the world will testify to this.

The option has to appeal as it is not a bad profit as your maintenance fee is only $500. So the $500 is paid and then you wait…..and wait…….you either receive a check in the post that will not clear, or you never hear from them again.

At this point you may be reading this and thinking to yourself there is no way that anyone could fall for this. Please don't laugh. Once you are put in this situation it is very hard to resist the temptation. Think about it, and remember there are many Timeshare Owners who do not use their Timeshare, have been trying to rent it for years and now they are finally being offered large amounts of money.

You have just been told you can get $2,000 for renting your Timeshare. Most of the time this figure is much, much higher. We are just trying to make it believable to you the reader. Figures as high as $5,000 are sometimes quoted. This is backed up to make it sound true with many different pitches like *"this is a high season week and we have a middle-eastern client"* or *"due to you owning a 2bed we list it as a sleep eight so we can charge per person."*

Paying a $500 fee seems so simple. It sounds a no brainier. For the Scam to pay out into millions the company probably would have bought a list of Timeshare Owners. As mentioned before it is not hard to purchase lists of millions of Timeshare owners and then set up a telesales operation. When you take $500 and multiply this by say 3,000 unsuspected Timeshare owners you get a seven figure sum. The company then disappears along with the funds and once again thousands of Timeshare Owners have being duped out of their money and are still trying to rent or sell their Timeshare.

IF THIS IS SUCH A GENUINE OFFER THEN THE COMPANY SHOULD DEDUCT THE $500 FROM THE $2,500 THEY HAVE PROMISED THAT THEY WILL RECEIVE AND THEN PAY YOU THE BALANCE!

This Scam can be flipped to a sales scam. The same style of cold-call which is a pre-call six months prior and then the urgency call that they have a buyer. Very similar to **Scam One** that we listed earlier, but no upfront fee, at least not yet anyway. That happens when they call to say they have managed to get $20,000 for the week. Please send the $500 administration/commission fee and they will take care of all closing and title changes.

TIMESHARE-SCAMS.ORG RECOMMENDS THE ONLY WAY TO SELL OR RENT YOUR TIMESHARE IS THROUGH A COMPANY THAT CHARGE NO UPFRONT FEES. SO AFTER READING THE ABOVE SCAM WHERE A COMPANY OFFERS TO RENT OR SELL YOUR TIMESHARE FOR NO UPFRONT FEE, WHO DO YOU BELIEVE?

First off, look for a company that has trading history. This scam is usually a quick target over a six month period, an "IN and OUT!" They set up a web site that looks professional, buy a list of a million Timeshare Owners and do a mammoth cold calling pitch knowing that the numbers game will work, and then they shut down and set up again under a different name.

You have to believe yourself. We can give you advice from the research we have done, but we also recommend you research yourself, this way we should come across the same facts. Speaking to existing Timeshare Owners that have been trying to sell their Timeshare, should give you fair advice from their experience.

The simple fact again is that you should not pay over huge amounts of funds on a promise or guarantee of selling or renting your Timeshare, or your money back. This message will be repeated many times throughout this book.

Scam 5

The reload scam. This is simply an amazing technique that plays with your mind. Now you don't get a call, you get a letter!!!!

By post you will receive a professional looking letter from a company to say they have SOLD your Timeshare, there will also be a check made out, in your name, for a substantial amount of money, for example $20,000. This is what the clever part is. For many people seeing and touching a check complete with all account numbers, sort codes and with your name as the payee, can feel quite dazzling. You have finally sold your Timeshare; the check is in your hand. So where is the con?

Well, to be able to cash the check you need to pay the tax due on the full amount of the check. This is why the amount of the check will be very high as then of course a higher rate of tax is due. The tax part is what makes this believable as you can completely understand that in all countries different tax rules apply, and for unpaid tax the punishments can be very hard.

So you're all happy and feeling safe as the letter itself is professionally written complete with testimonials from other Timeshare Owners and full instructions on what to do. (Another deceiving part will be that you will be given a deadline of seven to ten days to pay this tax due or all the funds will be withdrawn and you will lose the sale of your timeshare). This deadline often works and you send off the tax amount and go ahead and bank your check. The check will take a few weeks to finally clear, yet you have transferred the funds directly or given your credit card details and paid straight away. Here another few thousand dollars are paid out, and when the time comes for the check to clear it bounces and you are charged a fee from your bank. More money out of pocket and still stuck with the Timeshare you are so desperate to sell.

Another version of this Scam is very similar to a worldwide scam where you are sent a check for an amount much higher than the price you asked for your Timeshare, you might get a check for $30,000 when you were promised $20,000.

This will again be backed up with a very slick pitch about tax benefits or a loophole to save you money; all you need to do is to send back the difference. For your time and effort you can keep $1,000. So you send back $9,000 in real money and by the time you get to cash your $30,000 check the whole lot bounces and you are completely out of pocket.

Scam 6 (Can also be known as the Rescue Scam).

If you have fallen victim to any of the Timeshare Scams that we have or have not listed, you can expect a call from a company that claims to be only interested in protecting all Timeshare Owners and reclaim back any funds that have been taken from them under false promises. They must be telepathic, because they somehow know to always call just after you have paid money to a company, and been fraudulently deceived. This is what makes this Scam work, as it is all about timing. In the majority of cases you will be most vulnerable when you've just found out that you have been duped. When someone all of a sudden calls with an offer to help and get all of your monies back this can prove to be an irresistible proposal.

So completely out of the blue you get a phone call from a company claiming that they are chasing crooked Timeshare companies that have been taking money from people on the promise to sell or rent their Timeshare. How did they know to call you? Is it really pure chance? Or is it the same company operating under a different name? Or maybe they have just sold your details to someone else for a substantial fee?

These scripts are written to perfection as they will strangely coincide with exactly what has happened to you.

Let's say you have been hit by Scam One, the call may be:

"Good evening Mr. Johnson, we are from get your money back dot website and are calling to find out if you have recently paid money over to a Timeshare Company on the promise that they have a buyer for your week?"

"Yes"

"And please, let me ask, did the sale fail to go through so they promised a full refund if they did not find another buyer within 12 months"

"Why yes"

"Thank you Mr. Johnson we have been chasing this company for a long time. Were you invited to a presentation where someone offered to buy your week IF you bought theirs?"

Again now the unsuspected Timeshare Owner now feels safe as they seem to have found someone (they called you) who can relate to what happened to you.

"Mr. Johnson, I hate to say this but the company you dealt with were operating and doing business under false circumstances. Were they called xxxxxxx?"

Of course they even now know the company name, how much was taken and the style in the way it all happened.

"The good news Mr. Johnson is that you were not alone in this terrible incident. This has happened to thousands of others and we are now working with the local Police in bringing these criminal fraudsters to justice. We have managed to strike a deal with the office of fair trading and before this company is wound up and the owners are prosecuted and taken to court, which you know can delay any refunds of monies owed for a very long time, we can get all the monies you paid out refunded to you within the next 7 days."

"You can, oh well that is fantastic news"

"don't worry Mr. Johnson we are on the case, all we need is $300 (this fee could be more or less depending on how much you lost) to process all this. The fee is paid to the fair trading office to speed up your refund process and to save the time and cost of court proceedings."

The whole script will be re worded and changed to fit the client's situation at that time, the amount will vary depending on how much they feel they can squeeze out of you and this Scam can be associated with any of the Scams listed here, as well as many others.

It really is that convincing and many, many Timeshare Owners pay out again large sums of money only never to see it again. It's a double whammy only weeks after they were scammed before and can leave many feeling ill.

Another version that tends to happen a few months down the road, is where you are contacted about being scammed before by a certain company, and this time they say they have the full funds ready for you, but not just the amount you were scammed, but the whole amount that you originally paid for your Timeshare.

How can this happen? This has to be too good to be true?

Well due to some make believe world-wide Timeshare law that they create, your Timeshare gets repossessed and placed in the hands of the fraudulent company, and they become responsible for it.

This is why this Scam happens a few months later, as this time the Scammers will stake that they are operating on behalf of the government.

The script will go something like this…

"We are acting on behalf of the government and we believe a certain company xxxxxx have taken money

from you under false pretenses. Due to this, you will be eligible for a full refund of what was taken from you, plus a full refund of the price you paid for your Timeshare. As we are acting on behalf of the government, we are only to be paid once you receive your funds".

This will only be an initial call to confirm who you are and of course if you are interested in your refund. Who wouldn't?

Then you will get another call a week later to say everything is going ahead, they will e-mail or post you the agreement and could you provide them with your credit card details, to pay a handling charge fee, $500 to $750, once the payment has gone through.

You have guessed it, nothing happens and another lump sum leaves your bank account.

You, the reader, who has not had this happen to you, again must be thinking there is no way anyone could fall victim for this. It's a known fact that thousands have had this happen to them, in fact hundreds of thousands. Take $500 and times it by just 50,000. Innocent Timeshare Owners, this is a multimillion dollar Scam!

The companies are very convincing. They will state how they have got back money for hundreds of other Timeshare Owners and all this will be backed up with another professional looking website and many testimonials from Timeshare Owners who heave a sigh of relief and are so grateful for this company rescuing their thousands of dollars.

In most cases the only companies that can successfully get money back from Timeshare Owners that have been scammed, are the credit card companies or the banks themselves that the funds have been taken from.

There may be companies that offer a service to get money refunded back to Timeshare Owners that have been scammed, but surely this should be a service that is only paid for once the funds have been returned to the Owners? Just mentioning this can lead to Scams being created, very similar to Scam five, where you will get a check in the post with the amount that you had lost, just pay the tax (now a smaller amount and we will clear the check). Please be careful and make sure you get legal advice on what they are offering or again search Timeshare forums and research the company name that is offering this service.

We would love to hear of proven testimonials from Timeshare Owners that have been successful in regaining any monies that had been taken from them. This will give many people hope and we will be happy to share this information on our website. Please e-mail **info@timeshare-scams.org**

Scam 7

We now have a Scam where your Timeshare is actually stolen from you. How?

They steal your Ownership Certificate, forge signatures and low and behold your Timeshare is taken right off you and then sold on to some unsuspecting person at an unbelievably low price to sell quickly before any one catches up with them.

You get the usual telephone call from a company claiming to sell Timeshares. They will have another pre written script explaining how they have sold your week for $$$$$$$. This price will be a lot more than you expected. Sometimes not just double but even five times what you wanted. This will be made to sound very believable as they mention that they have clients in the Far East who need to get the money out of the country; to them this is peanuts and gives them a foothold abroad. Russia and China are countries mentioned. The closing line is that they do not ask for any money!!!!! They do not want any upfront fee!!!!! They do not want your credit card or bank details. They will deduct their fee from the buyer and send you the rest.

Now that does sound too good to be true. So what is the catch? Where is the scam?

The danger is that they ask you for your Ownership Certificate and the $$$$$$$$ will be sent to you in 14 days.

This sounds very simple and of course must be the right way to do business. They want you to prove you own the week and in order for the transaction to go through all you have to do is send them your Ownership Certificate.

You send out all the details of your Timeshare and then you wait…. and wait……….. and wait………….. Until eventually you call them and no one ever answers.

What has happened is that they have then changed your ownership details and gone and sold your Timeshare for whatever price they choose or rented it out. The benefit maybe that you have sold your Timeshare but for no money! You have given it away.

NEVER SEND YOUR OWNERSHIP TITLE TO ANYONE. ALWAYS USE A CLOSING COMPANY.

At this stage we would like to introduce Timeshare Closing Agents and the use of Escrow accounts. Timeshare Closing Agents will act on your behalf (for a fee) when it comes to the legal transaction of funds and ownership certificates when selling your Timeshare. Many of the companies that call you and operate these scams will tell you they will take care of all of this on your behalf; they will even pick up the fee. You would not sell your House this way so do not sell your Timeshare this way. Use a professional closing agent that specializes in Timeshare. Again these are pretty easy to find and by speaking to Timeshare Owners on forums who have successfully sold their Timeshare you should get some recommendations.

Scam 8

This is a simple scam that in a way puts the Rescue Scam together with another Scam and is usually an additional way to squeeze a little bit more out of an already duped Timeshare Owner. For example, the Timeshare Owner six months ago may have paid $400 to a Timeshare Company who had promised to sell their Timeshare. Next, they get a call from a 2ⁿᵈ Timeshare Company who offers to sell their week for them at a special promotion that they have running in America or the Far East. Any country they choose. The fee they need is $350.

The Timeshare Owner explains that they have already registered with another Timeshare company.

"That's ok Mr. Johnson, all Timeshare Companies work under the new Timeshare Trades act (whatever that is) and when we sell your week for you we can get a full refund of the fee the other company has charged you. Give us the companies' details and we can start this process now. Do you own a 2 bed in Florida?

You do, fantastic, that area at present is in the highest demand for resale in the Far East, they just love Orlando, and see great value in resale instead of direct from the developer. We sold over $1,000,000 of Florida resale Timeshare last month!!!!!!"

That, or words to that effect, is an example of a script that will be used on the unsuspecting Timeshare Owner who really wants to sell their week.

Pretty hard to resist isn't it?

Hopefully now you can understand why the thought of paying a small fee of $350 makes sense. Remember you have been told your week will sell, at a profit and your other fee will be refunded.

A high percentage of the time, the fee is paid, it turns out this company calling you really is the same company that called you before just under a different name and now they have $750 out of you and you still own the Time-share!

Scam 9

A very worrying Scam that sounds very professional and is backed by companies with fancy names, gold seals and professional letter headed paper.

Again this will start with a phone call or even a very professional letter with the heading…..

Can't Sell Your Timeshare? Then convert it into a money back guaranteed bond.

The call, or letter, states that you will be guaranteed your money back. It is very simple, give us your Timeshare plus $3,000 and you will get back the original price that you paid for your Timeshare in so many months time. The Time-share Owner hands over their ownership certificate and the money and in return get a very important looking bond with the words:

44

Guaranteed repayment to Mr. & Mrs. Johnson on 1st January 2010

2010 January 1st comes and what happens? Nothing! The company has long gone, with your $3,000 and your Timeshare.

This Scam is very professional and is very convincing. The bond in some cases will be backed by a government and most likely be based in a tax free country. The bond may end up being worth as little as $100.

Scam 10

There have been reports of a new Scam where companies relieve the Timeshare Owner of their Timeshare. As you may expect, after reading all the above scams some Timeshare Owners prefer just to be free of their Timeshare and the ongoing costs. So when they get a call again, unexpectedly (how do these companies know you want to sell?) with the offer to take your Timeshare off your hands, this again is an easy sell to the crooks.

The script will be professional, sleek and smooth. Somehow they have your details and know you are keen to sell. They offer to relieve you of your Timeshare and all future payments that would be due. This is done by you paying them a fee to assume financial responsibility of your Timeshare and the company will recoup that fee by using the amount as a deduction on their federal taxes in the coming year. The fee will usually be approximately five years worth of your maintenance fee. Backed up like other Scams with a professional looking website and many testimonials from happy Timeshare Owners relieved to be rid of their Timeshare. The clever pitch is that this company does not sell or buy Timeshares, they persuade owners to pay them to take responsibility for the Timeshare.

The Timeshare Owner wants complete freedom of their Timeshare and this looks an easy way that will stop any annual fees being charged to them in the future. The only issue is that months down the road the fees are still due and the Timeshare is still theirs, except this time that they are monies out of pocket due to a crooked scam.

You have just read some of the most popular Scams that have and still are being used to cheat Timeshare Owners out of money. We have to add as well, that these Scams do not stop at just a phone call, a letter or a postcard to your home.

You will find, and this will not be a complete shock, that there are Timeshare Scams which are actually used at a Timeshare presentation. Unfortunately, Timeshare presentations are notorious for high pressure sales tactics and repeated use of false promises. All of this can mean some Scams start immediately after your first purchase.

The obvious ones are where you are completely given the wrong impression about how you can use the Timeshare you are buying. Hence, when you discover this a few months on from your purchase, the first thing you wish to do is sell your Timeshare. As we have stated, Timeshare can be an amazing product which can give memorable vacations all over the world. Yet, it is a shame that you will find a very high number of the Owners who wish to sell their Timeshare because they were misrepresented when they first bought.

Most of the lies you will hear at a Timeshare presentation are…

The fees do not go up!

Exchanges are very easy and you can always go where you want! (Exchanges can be very easy but it is not easy to swap a studio in low season for a 2 bed at a ski resort in the high season. A 2 bed in Cape Cod in January may not get you a swap to Hawaii at Christmas).

If at any stage you decide that you do not want your Timeshare, you can sell it very quickly at a huge profit! (This can be re-worded to *"We will buy it back from you"*).

You tend to hear these statements at only a few of the Timeshare presentations world-wide, mainly with companies that usually disappear six months down the road or from rogue sales individuals who work at so many different Timeshare Companies that they move on before they are caught out.

All of the professional respectable Timeshare Companies in the world sell their products under the Timeshare Law. This is where you are given, by Law, a cooling off period from the day you sign. Cooling off period meaning, the right to cancel the agreement within a certain period of time and a full refund of any monies paid.

The length of the cooling off period does vary from country to country, but it does exist. It exists for a very good reason. Not just so you can buy and then cancel, more so that if you find that you have been misrepresented in any sort of way then you can get out, and be refunded your deposit. Remember, only to do business with companies that follow this law.

Scam 11

A very mischievous scam which can easily be used as a ***"well we did promise that but it's not our fault that the market changed"*** style of pitch.

You are at a Timeshare presentation and you have been sold a Timeshare on the promise, or may we say guarantee that Your Timeshare will be rented out every year. For example, you are sold the Timeshare for $10,000 but are presented that you do not have to use it as they will rent it for you for $2,000 plus every year. This pays your fee and gives you a nice income of profit on top, which most of the time will cover your monthly payments for the finance plan they sell you. In simple terms, the Timeshare pays for itself

48

in fewer than ten years. You are getting it for free!!!! That has to be an irresistible offer.

Though this sounds great, in many cases guaranteed rental does not exist. If this is presented to you and you decide to purchase, based on these facts, make sure that you are given time to leave and research this information. Timeshare is a product that can be rented, and many Timeshare Owners world-wide are very successful at renting at a good profit. The Scam is if you are sold a Timeshare purely on the basis that it will be "guaranteed".

Scam 12

The buy-sell is a very old scam that is hardly used on the sales decks of the world now, but there are a few that still operate this awful crime. It's a classic example of touching on the greed of someone's mind and then of course providing a very tempting offer. To set the scene, imagine that you are the Timeshare Owner who owns a 2bed condo for a week that you bought a few years ago for say $7,500. You have been invited to a presentation with the offer of a 3 night stay at reduced price or maybe you are on vacation and a few tickets to the park make you agree to give up 90minutes of your time. Anyway, you are on a presentation and you have no intention of buying as you already own.

The sales rep does his pitch; you mention that you are a Timeshare Owner already. The rep says no problem and continues on with the fantastic presentation that of course you have to agree is a very nice Timeshare to own, yet you give your reason for not buying.

"Thank you for a great presentation you really have explained it well but unfortunately we already own a Timeshare. Maybe if we had not bought already we may have considered buying this one."

That is a typical line given by a Timeshare Owner choosing not to buy.

Then the buy-sell kicks in, they ask for the name of the resort you own and how much you paid, off they go to the back office and a manager comes to your table.

"Mr. and Mrs. Johnson, or may I call you John and Mary?
I understand you own a 2 bed red week at a very nice resort by the beach. I don't know if the sales rep mentioned this before, but we are also agents for our Timeshare Company that have 16 offices in Eastern Europe and Asia. There has been a massive increase in Timeshare resales in this market since the curtain came down and people now have the option of travelling world-wide. If you don't mind I am just going to give a call to our office, as only last week there was a client who owned at the same resort as you, that sold his week for $16,500."

This is re worded in many ways to fit the scene at the table but you get the message, the manger goes off and calls this make believe Asian office, comes back and says *"you are in luck, they have a waiting list for your week, you can't get $16,500 but if you are willing to go ahead*

***now we can guarantee you $15,000 if you purchase our
$8,000 Timeshare here."***

The Timeshare owner is promised $15,000 into their bank a/c within 14 days from getting home, this will give them their money back on what they paid plus enough to buy this new Timeshare that unfortunately they have claimed to have interest in. They are then asked to put down a $2,000 deposit to secure everything and the clever bit is they then hear words like,

***"Look John and Mary, we are putting a lot of trust
in you. Please, as soon as you get home, can you fax a
copy of proof of your ownership so we can get this off to
our Asian office as soon as possible?"***

The tables are turned; the clients do not want to miss out on this amazing offer. THEY HAVE BEEN TOLD THEY CAN SELL THEIR TIMESHARE FOR DOUBLE WHAT THEY PAID. The credit card comes out, they pay the deposit and spend the next fourteen days all excited about the money they have made and this brand new Timeshare they own. As you can guess two weeks later nothing happens, the deal falls through.

They have two options, lose the $2,000 they paid as a deposit or pay the balance remaining on what they owe, hoping they can sell it. They now own two Timeshares. This of course leads to them wanting to now sell one of them and they enter the Timeshare Resale market and are introduced to the world of many of the scams we have listed here. It really goes full circle time and time again.

Scam 13

There you have a few of the scams that can happen at a Timeshare Sales Presentations. You have been provided a good list of potential scams to stay away from and you have been warned that you could be contacted by phone, post or even at a presentation. To complete the list we have to include e-mail. To the scammers, this is the easy way and with today's technology they can keep targeting Timeshare Owners all of the time. We know of this first hand as we were e-mailed on our Timeshare-scam email an offer to help sell our Timeshare that we have listed on craigslist!

We of course are NOT selling a Timeshare on craigslist with a contact e-mail of Timeshare-scams, yet this showed us that whatever technology that these scammers are using, it is all about just targeting e-mail addresses. Computer systems can be set up to send millions of emails every day, and all can be automated.

Be warned of this though, because unbeknown to you, it can be very easy for professional hackers to collect e-mail address and many companies will "sell-on" their customer database list. Millions of Timeshare owners will have filled in their e-mail address after attending a presentation or after staying at a Timeshare resort, so it will not be hard to collect this data.

This is a copy of the e-mail we received, of course with company names taken out.

Dear future client!

I noticed that you had your timeshare for sale / rent on craigslist. Any luck yet?

Take a look at our website and fill out the contact form if you're interested in hearing more about our program. Our company gets a 6% finders fee after the sale of your property!

We are also excepting clients in our refund your money back program!! We can, and will, help you to obtain refunds from any company you've paid within the last year to help you sell your timeshare!!

Please visit us at "this is a complete scam .website"

Thank you for your time and consideration!

That has many of the scams we have listed all in one simple e-mail. It's amazing to be told that they **CAN** and **WILL** help you obtain refunds from any company you've paid within the last year to help sell your Timeshare.

That's the clever line of course; they can and will help you. I wonder what helping you will mean? Maybe they will send a few e-mails?

Send an e-mail like that to one million plus Timeshare owners and hope someone gets sucked in. In most cases just .5 of a % is 5,000, take that and the $500 fee they want and you have a nice tidy sum for a quick e-mail and a fancy website.

Sorry we forgot to mention the $500 fee. Yet they mention in their e-mail that they take a finders fee after the sale of your Timeshare.

We of course visit their site and get to see a website with many fancy looking pictures and many of the top brand names of Timeshare being listed for sale. We feel we have a pretty good experience of the Timeshare market, and, at a quick look at these resorts, we find that some of the pictures they use do not even match the resorts that they go with!

In addition though to gain your trust, they have a copy of the contract they wish you to enter. Have a real good read of this, many unsuspecting Timeshare Owners have signed and paid monies to companies that operate in this way.

THESE ARE THE ABOVE TERMS AND CONDITIONS OF CONTRACT

1.   *xxxxxxxxxxx will charge a 6% Finders Fee AFTER the sale of your property.*
2.   *xxxxxxxxxxxxxxx is an advertising company and is not a real estate broker. The advertising fee is for marketing expenses that pool advertising resources with those of other sellers and renters to maximize exposure. xxxxxxxxxxxxxx helps our clients sell and rent their property without a commission.*
3.   *Xxxxxxxxxxxxx will forward all inquires in writing, email, or by phone directly to me. The*

negotiation, sale or rental of my timeshare unit will not involve any brokers or commission fees.

4. *xxxxxxxxxxxxxx is NOT involved in any of the negotiations for the sale or rental of my timeshare unit and it is up to me (the client) to accept or decline the offer.*

5. *xxxxxxxxxxxxx assumes that my timeshare unit sells or rents within 6 months. Right of cancellation is seven days from the date of contract agreement/transaction agreement.*

6. *xxxxxxxxxxxxxxx, at our discretion, will advertise your timeshare in newspapers, magazines, billboards, the internet and our daily marketing booths for a 6 month period.*

7. *If the seller / leaser does not receive any reasonable offers to sell their property within 6 months from the time that the property is listed, the above seller / lesser can apply for a FULL REFUND.*

8. *Enclosed is my CHECK or MONEY ORDER made payable to xxxxxxxxxxxx or authorization to charge my Major Credit Card.*

It disgusts us that a contract like this is made to a Timeshare Owner, with the clever words that they "CAN apply for a full refund if you do not receive any offers for your Timeshare within six months". Just like Scam One we listed, you will get an offer, it may be only if you purchase a separate Timeshare or it may just be so low you refuse it. Realistically you can say goodbye to your Full refund.

We have the right to add this agreement to this book as this clever company decided to e-mail Timeshare Scams with the offer to sell our Timeshare for us, we have the e-mail to prove it, and it gives us great pleasure to share this with our readers. This is an advertising company that will list your Timeshare for sell or rent.

AGAIN THERE ARE MANY PROFESSIONAL TIME-SHARE RESALE COMPANIES THAT WILL PROVIDE A VERY GOOD SERVICE FOR ANY TIMESHARE OWNER WHO WISHES TO SELL THEIR TIMESHARE AND THEY DO NOT HAVE TO PROMISE YOU YOUR MONEY BACK IF IT DOES NOT SELL OR CLAIM TO GET MONEY BACK FOR YOU.

You, the Timeshare Owner, have the right to choose how you wish to advertise your Timeshare for sale. As we keep mentioning, make sure you do your research first.

While we are on the subject of Timeshare Owners being scammed we would like to warn any potential buyers of Timeshare of another Scam which is being used all over the world. This is a Scam where you have companies pretending to be Timeshare Resale Brokers who list quality branded Timeshares for sale at very low prices. The Timeshare is at a great price, the problem is when the buyer pays the money and gets nothing in return, except, perhaps a photocopy of an ownership certificate in the name of someone else. Some of these certificates are forgeries.

Many of these companies will carry the logo of a trade body in order to give themselves credibility. The trade body concerned only exists as a few words on a piece of paper and no reliance should be given to such traders.

It is disturbing, and very sad, to believe that the Scams we have listed have conned thousands of Timeshare Owners out of millions of dollars. We hope that after reading this it may save some of the six million Timeshare Owners, thousands in the future! Please make sure this information is shared with anyone you know who owns a Timeshare as well. Pass our website details to any friends or family that own Timeshare, so they can be warned of any new scams that enter the Timeshare world. **www.timeshare-scams.org**

Testimonials from Owners

In our research, while writing this book, we received Testimonials from Timeshare Owners who have been scammed in some way or another, when it came to the selling or renting of their Timeshare. You can read thousands of others on the internet at various Timeshare forums. We have selected two that really stood out and we hope that as these are written by genuine Timeshare Owners who were scammed, the message may hit home to you the reader at how unfortunate it can be for the Timeshare Owner. Or depending on how you view it, how misleading and deceiving these scammers can be.

When we say scammed, this means that they were promised that their Timeshare would be rented or sold for a sum of money and that, if this did not happen, any fees they paid would be fully refunded. Or the Timeshare Owners paid out money in advance under false promises of a quick sell or some guarantee of a return that never happened.

The first was an innocent Timeshare Owner from the United Kingdom; he finally caved in after weeks of phone calls.

"To Timeshare-scams.org,

We never had any intention of selling our Timeshare. Okay we were not using it as much as we wanted and maybe this made us weaker when we finally gave in after weeks of phone calls, but we were quite happy with our one week of Timeshare every year.

Still it all started with these constant phone calls. Nearly every night just after we had finished dinner and were sitting down watching TV the phone would ring and a voice at the end would say, *"Good evening is that Mr. McMillan?"* They would know our name and even what Timeshare we owned. How excited we were, as they promised that we could sell our Timeshare for thousands more then we paid, and that they even had buyers lined up. When I say thousands more, we had paid just over £10,000 for our week in Florida and had owned it for about 10 years. Anyway, these calls started and really, we just ignored them, we were not attracted to selling and we did not believe what they said anyway. On every call we listened to their pitch out of politeness, we tried to say that they were wasting their time and just kept repeating how we were not interested.

The calls though, did not stop. We would get different voices claiming to be from different companies, but I always felt it was the same office; the noise in the background always sounded the similar. It was funny, on one call, I was watching the football and actually just had the phone sitting by my ear saying *"ummm"* and *"really"* every few minutes, while this salesman did his fifteen minute plus sales pitch. We would have not answered if we knew who they were but their number never showed up on our caller ID.

They do say that persistence works and I don't know if it is all about timing or just that we gave in but I was having a rough time at work, a few bills had come in and we decided that we were not going on holiday that year yet were still paying our maintenance fee. We got a call and the voice was completely different to before, a young girl this time and maybe she just had the right temperament, but whatever she did she won me over, she mentioned how our resort was becoming very popular with the Chinese who were looking at taking holidays in Orlando. They were travelling more now than ever and saw Timeshare as great value as they normally travelled as a large family. They had a waiting list of people wanting to buy our Timeshare and had just opened an office in Beijing to cope with the demand. Anyone who reads this will say I was stupid, but she 100% guaranteed us a full refund if our Timeshare did not sell. The refund was for the £500 fee that they wanted a fee we only found out about right at the end. This was an advertisement fee that they charged to cover the heavy TV, radio and internet advertising that they did. I said "but you have a buyer?" to which she explained *"yes but only after all the advertising that we have done, we do not charge any commissions so you keep the whole amount once it is sold."* Again it sounded quiet believable so I asked her to call me back tomorrow, this gave me time to check their website and talk to my wife.

My wife and I discussed it, she was not too keen but I had been on the call and felt all was good. It's funny, I had a feeling deep inside that we were being conned here but the thought of the 20,000 pounds they claimed we would receive kept out weighing the thought of the 500 pounds we may lose if it does not sell, still don't forget we were promised our money back!

The following night, right on time she called. I had a few questions but they were all answered to my satisfaction, and I said go ahead. I gave my credit card details, paid the money, and looked forward to the money I was to receive. This process was to take about 6 weeks, due to some regulations in China to register our week for sale there. It sounded good and was very believable what they said. A few days later some documents came in the post which we signed and provided proof of our ownership. It was funny now we had taken the plunge even though I read the small print that our fee is only refunded if we do not receive any offers for our week, it all sounded believable and trustworthy to me. The paperwork was all smart and professional looking and included a few testimonials from other happy Timeshare Owners who had successfully sold their Timeshare. I wanted to sell my Timeshare, and I was being offered "double" what I paid, they had been calling me for months and I thought it was worth the risk. I WAS WRONG. And I write this letter in the hope that others will not fall prey and become victims to this scam. About 10 weeks passed and I called their office. This time the sweet young lady didn't answer or return my calls. I was told no one else could help me as she was dealing with my Timeshare. On one call I was told she was in China. Then she called to say they had sold my week but the offer was a lot less, the original buyer had pulled out for personal reasons but someone had offered 4,000 pounds for our week. After all that she had promised, I refused, saying how this was a con and a scam. Right there I had lost my fully refundable fee. Looking back at the paperwork they could have offered me just 10 pounds for our Timeshare. The paperwork says that I loose my fee if we do not receive any offers, well what is an offer?

It is over a year since all that happened. We still get the calls from all different companies, now we get more and have thought about changing our number, but then why should we let these crooks affect our family and friends, we just put the phone down straight away and say no thanks. We learnt the hard way. We have never told anyone of our mistake, we do feel embarrassed, but maybe it was greed that took us over! Or is it maybe that just like a child keeps asking you, and asking you, then maybe the persistence that came from these callers finally wore us down. In my defense it was the fully refundable fee "fully guaranteed". Still that was worthless. We cannot claim anything back, we signed the paperwork and we paid the money. It's

one of those things you put down to experience and you certainly don't tell people. Again please feel free to share this letter with your readers. Don't pay any money upfront no matter how good it sounds.

"Keep up the good work"

There you have a letter from an innocent Timeshare Owner who some may feel was foolish to fall victim to this scandalous act of deceit. But we hope after reading his letter that maybe you will see that he was being pushed so much, that finally he gave in.

Remember these are not shops in your local mall that you can choose to visit or not. The scammers approach you! By phone, post or e-mail, and they do not stop at all. They have found by constant bombardment, over and over again, that it is only a matter of time before an innocent few will cave in. Just like the selling of Timeshare, it's a numbers game, it's percentages, and if you have a list of over a million Timeshare Owners to target as long as a small percentage fall victim, they are making a substantial profit. This runs into millions of dollars.

Our second letter shows a different style of deceit. Here we have a Timeshare Owner who wanted to sell, so started to do research to find a Timeshare company to assist him.

" Here are a few candid comments on my experiences trying to sell my Timeshare at the xxxxxx Beach Club, in xxxxxxxxxx

I listed the property with a person named xxxxxx xxxxx at www.xxxxxx He was one of several who called me after I began to do some inquiring of services on the internet. He was actually the nicest of the 6 or 7 people who called...soft spoken....from FL....retired minister....family man....very soft approach vs. the pushy approach others used. Said he knew the property well and that it was an easy sell at a listing of $24,995. He said several others had recently sold in that range (I did not confirm this, and that was a miss on my part!).

I paid $20,000 for the property in 10/94. He said that for a fee of $1,995 that he would give an exclusive listing for 120 days as one of their featured properties and then if it hadn't sold it would go on their regular listing for an unlimited time until the property closed. I would pay no commissions and no closing fees. The market was selling well and this would be an easy one to sell. It was listed under ad # xxxxxxx

Almost 2 years later the property has not sold. I've lowered the price to $16,000 and spoken with xxxx xxxxx twice in the interim 2 year period. In both cases he was always too busy to talk but my persistence wore him down I guess. I have a call in to him now because I can't even find a listing for my property. Perhaps you can find it? If you do, please let me know.

This was obviously a mistake on my part. I've always believed in the goodness of people and the soft approach used by the salesman misled me. I should have done more research on the guy, the Timeshare Company and the resort itself, who would have confirmed actual property sales of units like mine. If you recall, when you called, the units like mine were selling in the $16,000 range.

The lesson learned...do your homework on the company. I was taken in by the soft believable approach. I was naïve and ignorant...and it cost me. Also, do your own research on unit resales in the property. There's no way a unit like mine sold for $24k!!!!

Hope this helps. I'm angry.....at the reseller...and myself.

I'm still interested in renting or selling the property. Maybe you can advise or help?

Best regards"

You can read how angry this Timeshare Owner is. As he says, not just at the reseller but at himself for not doing any further research. But is it his fault? He was only listening to what was promised; why not believe what was being told. These companies represent themselves as professional and experienced in the Timeshare world.

We have since, stepped in on behalf of the Timeshare Owner, to assist him with the selling of his week, advising him on where to advertise his week for FREE and also a much more realistic price to list it for. If you would like free advice on the selling or renting of your Timeshare then e-mail help@timeshare-scams.org

REASONS FOR SELLING YOUR TIMESHARE

If, as we have stated many times in this book that Timeshare is an amazing product, providing nearly six million individuals and families outstanding vacations all over the world, why is there such a high number of owners wanting to sell their Timeshare?

Let's share some of the main reasons.

Need Cash

Half way through our research, and writing of this book, the shocking story of The Global Financial Crisis that was emerging, became major news. The media was dominated by dreadful stories of the failure of United States based financial firms and the insolvency of many large corporations throughout the world. Recession and words like Credit Crunch became the main topics of conversation, topped off with declining stock market prices around the globe which has caused many pensions to lose their value.

There have been worldwide job losses, and even unemployment has reached its highest level for over a quarter of a century, along with the housing market taking big hits with many homes decreasing in value. As it has shown before, everything picks up in the end; it just takes time, yet in a panic situation many Timeshare Owners are looking to sell.

If you are ever in a cash shortfall, then your pleasure items tend to be the first that are sold. By selling your Timeshare you can free yourself of your annual fees and also recoup some of your initial outlay.

Sold the wrong product!

This is a main cause behind many owners wishing to sell their Timeshare. They were sold the Timeshare on the promise of what it can do, only to find out the complete opposite. The facts are that Trading Power does exist. A low season week in Branson will not always get you New Years Eve in the Caribbean, and you do need a high number of points to get a peak season vacation in a 3 bed apartment.

Just to get the sale you will find many presentations that tend to extend the truth. You can be promised the world and it may look just too irresistible, so it is awkward to say no. The monthly payments are affordable and if it does what it says, then of course it makes sense to buy. Yet that is why a cooling off period exists. So you have the opportunity to research what was told to you, speak to other Timeshare Owners who have bought and used what you are buying.

Timeshare does not need to be sold by exaggerated truth. It will do what it says, but of course you should be flexible. Many Timeshare Owners find out though that it was just not as flexible as they were told it would be. In most cases it's not that the product does not work, it's that they bought the $2,000 to $10,000 Timeshare in the low season at Cape Cod or Spain on the promise that they could swap it into the $20,000 to $30,000 Timeshares at peak resorts in ski season or school vacations. Where this can work sometimes, you are never guaranteed this and after a few years patiently waiting and getting frustrated of making requests that never happen, they decide to sell.

Fees have gone up too high?

This again can be out of your control and perhaps the fees that are due at your property have gone up too high, or raised a lot more than you were told when you first purchased. Some Timeshare Owners are never told that the fees will rise, or are promised that the increase will be so small that they have no need to worry......Then January comes and the maintenance fee has gone up 15%. This again can cause Timeshare Owners to think the worst, predicting a high increase in fees over the next few years, so they decide to sell. This is a difficult subject to discuss. In the defense though of Timeshare Owners who have seen a dramatic increase in their yearly fees since they have bought, it will only concern them of what it will cost in the years to come. With this worry they decide it may be best to sell their Timeshare

If, at the point of sale, the Buyer has been told information different to the facts, like fees never go up, then of course every Timeshare Owner has the right to be concerned about the future and what else they may have not been told. So once again instead of a Timeshare being used and enjoyed to its full potential, it goes unused and listed on the Resale market. If only the facts would have been told at the presentation, then maybe thousands of Timeshares would be being used and enjoyed, instead of being listed for sale.

In addition to this, to continue on from the effect of the Global Financial Crisis, this has seen many of the world's currencies devalue. This has another effect in what Timeshare Owners are paying every year. The hardest hit has been the UK Timeshare market with many owning Timeshare in the United States and Europe and the pound has lost a lot of value against the dollar and euro. For a typical two week Timeshare Owner paying two maintenance fees yearly, then they have seen quite a high increase. Of course this can change over time but again it has led to an increase in Timeshare Owners listing their ownership for sale.

Want a different resort?

Just like you move house due to a change in circumstances, Timeshare Owners that have owned at the same resort for many years may feel like a change and the thought of owning at a different resort appeals. For example the children may have left home and that Orlando Timeshare does not appeal anymore. Maybe they have been skiing most years but as they get older the idea of a "beach front" more relaxing Timeshare appeals.

You can also add that many owners wish to upgrade or downsize. The kids maybe choose not to take vacations with Mom and Dad anymore so the three bed that sleeps ten is just too big. Or they own a two bed but now grandchildren are on the scene and they need more space when going on vacation. This is the most positive part of the Timeshare Resale business where some great deals can be found from genuine sellers at fantastic Timeshare resorts.

There are many Timeshare Owners that want to sell their Timeshare so they can buy another one at a different location, and that location could be yours.

Lack of Use

A simple reason for owners wanting to sell their Timeshare is that they are just not using it anymore. This happens and is a plain and simple fact. Lifestyles change and the way they used to take vacations is different to the way they go now.

Through lack of use, you can ask an Owner where they own, and some cannot even remember the name of the resort they bought.

"It's something beach club in Cabo san Lucas" or **"I think it's called Fairway Bunkers Tennis Club, I don't know, we have not used it for years we just bank it and now are losing weeks we do not use."**

Words to that effect will often be heard from a Timeshare Owner who does not use their ownership anymore. They bought it years ago, never use it and just pay the fee every year. Usually the price paid for this Timeshare was so small that it is not even noticed anymore, but do remember if the price you paid was small, then the price that you should expect to sell it for should not be much higher.

Personal circumstances

This can be marriage break-up, a death in the family; there can be many personal reasons. And that's what they are, personal reasons. You own the Timeshare you have the right to sell it.

Receive constant bombardment of phone-call's, postcards and e-mails with the promise of a huge profit if you sell your Timeshare

This is what we have discussed and is the main topic of this book. Many owners do not wish to sell their Timeshare but after a slick marketing and a deceiving sales pitch with the promise of huge profits they soon end up joining the never ending list of Timeshares for sale.

If you take out the last option and you have not been cold-called and really want to sell your Timeshare. The area where you can get most misled is when it comes to finding what is the true resale value of your Timeshare?

WHAT IS MY TIMESHARE WORTH?

What is your Timeshare worth? This really is a difficult subject to talk about and a subject that is the cause of most of the Timeshare Scams that happen world-wide.

To be told that your Timeshare is worth thousands more than you paid can be quite uplifting news, but just because you have been told it is worth thousands more does not mean it will sell for thousands more.

When it comes to selling, you really need to decide the minimum price that you would accept back for your Timeshare and then aim that little bit higher leaving room to negotiate. But just like when you sell your home, you have to look at the current market prices to make sure you are within a range that will attract potential buyers. Unfortunately this is where you will see Timeshares priced as low as $1,000 and as high as $20,000 it all depends what the seller is looking for. And when you have a Timeshare priced at $10,000 and someone else is selling theirs for only $1,000, this really highlights the inconsistent world of Timeshare Resale's.

If you were to do an internet search on the Timeshare that you own and how much it is advertised for sale, it is highly likely that you will see pages of listings with your Timeshare selling at completely different prices.

Through no fault of your own, and just because of current market conditions, you could have nearly a hundred Timeshares listed for sale at the same resort and the same time of ownership, all at different prices.

You may have a quality Timeshare and it's genuine resale price could be $10,000, but if you have someone else who, due to personal financial circumstances, wants to sell the same Timeshare as quick as possible so lists it for as low as $1,500 this has just completely devalued what you own. How does this help the other Timeshare Owner who has been advised that their Timeshare has gone up in value and will sell for $20,000?

In any selling environment the lowest price will get more enquires. You may have Timeshare Owners out of work or maybe going through a divorce so just want to sell at any price and fast. This will not help you when you are listing your Timeshare for sale. Search the internet and you will see for yourself the thousands of Timeshares for sale, with such a high variation in price. You have to ask yourself how you can be promised that your Timeshare will sell, when some Timeshare companies charge you an upfront fee, then list your Timeshare for sale along with hundreds of others, all at different prices? If you know of any fellow Timeshare Owners who have tried to sell this way, ask them how many genuine enquires they have had. Have they sold? And at what price?

What price you sell your Timeshare for will first though come down to a few key points, and this is very similar to selling a home.

Location

This plays a big part. The desirability of where you're Timeshare is located. A beach front Timeshare with ocean views would be expected to command a higher price than a Timeshare in an urban location overlooking a busy road. But then of course it would all depend on who you are marketing. There may be a potential buyer who wants a Timeshare in an urban location and view is unimportant.

If your Timeshare is in Aruba then you can target a customer who wants to visit Aruba every year. If your Timeshare is in Orlando then target families wanting to visit the parks. You will always hear how important location is; yet if your feel your Timeshare is not in a highly desirable location do not be disheartened, as you just need to make sure it appeals to the right clients that take vacations where your Timeshare is.

A key point to remember is a high percentage of people buying Timeshare on the resale market look at buying the Timeshare to use at that location more often than exchange.

What Size

Did you know that less than 15% of the Timeshares in the world are three or four bedroom? If you own a three or a four bedroom then you can set your price higher as there is less demand. Or even if you own a one bedroom use this to your advantage and only target couples. Plus, remember with a one bedroom your maintenance fees will be lower. Two bedroom two bathrooms are the most common of all Timeshares with over 60% of the Timeshare market; hence Location and Season of a Two bedroom will push your price higher.

What Season

Your Timeshare may be a red week which can exchange world-wide but a lot of customers who purchase a Timeshare resale buy it to use at the property only, hence the time of year that your Timeshare can be used at your home resort is very important. Do you own a fixed week which can only be used at your home resort a set time of year? Is it a floating week? Owning a week that can be used at Christmas or New Year or the School vacations all play a big role in the price you can expect to receive for selling or renting your Timeshare.

We are mentioning words like red week, floating week, this Timeshare talk is unknown to some. For a full list of Timeshare terminology please use the guide at the back of this book.

View

Just like location, view makes a difference. Timeshares can be sold with a fixed view of Ocean or Golf course. You have to make sure you have the facts here. Do you own a fixed unit which guarantees the same unit every year?

Units

How many Timeshares units are there at the resort? A Timeshare resort with 900 units will not create such as high demand as a smaller boutique style resort with less than 100. We understand that this may sound like common sense to most people but it is important that we present the facts. Many Timeshare Owners are misled. When contacted about selling they may question that they own at a resort with over 1,000 other units, and have seen some that are being sold for $25,000 and some as low as $5,000.

"Don't worry Mrs. Jones, we have had many enquires for your Resort and are very confident that you will get at least $20,000. Seeing as you paid only $15,000 that is not a bad return. If you pay our $500 premium listing fee this should sell in days not weeks."

TIMESHARE-SCAM WARNING!

Please note, there will be Timeshare Companies that will have obtained details of Timeshare Owners who wish to sell. Prior to calling them they will place false adverts on their site with very inflated prices of the same Timeshare's for sale. Of course, when they call you and explain that the Timeshare you own is selling for thousands of dollars more than you paid, and if you do not believe them, then just visit their website

and see for yourself. This can be a very misleading yet powerful way to get people excited.

There is a flip side to this as there are many false adverts placed on Timeshare Resale websites at very, very low prices. And if this is the same Timeshare you own then it will straight away de value yours. The main reason for these ridiculously low prices is to get potential purchases to call in, looking to buy. Of course, when they call, it has actually just been sold, but don't worry, as they do have other Timeshares for sale. This leads into a very smooth sales pitch of selling another Timeshare, which of course is at a higher price.

Amenities

Does it come with free golf? Or any other perks? This is your big plus. If there are any amenities that the owners get to use free of charge, or at a discounted price, make sure you build this into your listing. This will also help with renting. Most resorts have free use of pools and gymnasiums, but many others offer park ticket discounts or reduced fees at local golf courses, some even with free golf. For example, you may be on a listing with hundreds of other Timeshares in Orlando, yet if yours comes with discount golf or park tickets when you are staying at the resort, yours will of course offer more appeal.

Do you own a Timeshare week or Points? Both of these offer different advantages. Is it a deeded property or a lease? Make sure you mention everything, as anything you do not mention will only re appear when it comes to the closing of the sale. For example, make sure all your fees are paid to date. If you have finance on the Timeshare, is it private or with the company you bought from; does the loan have to be paid in full before you can sell?

As we have said before, a lot of customers buying a resale, buy to use at the property. Key points to build in are,

Beach –year round
Beach – Seasonal
Island
Ski/Mountain
Desert
Country/Lakes
Rural/Coast
Urban

Geographic
North America
Latin America
Caribbean
Europe
Middle East & Africa
Asia
South Pacific

We can understand that to most this may sound all too complicated, hence why there are many Timeshare Companies that offer a service to sell your Timeshare for you. Of course they should charge you a fee for this service and we hope that the information that we have provided to warn you of potential scams will be enough to make sure you do not have to pay a ridiculous price on the promise of a guaranteed sale.

As we have done for past Timeshare Owners who have sent in testimonials telling us of how they have been scammed, if you need help in or advice regarding the selling or renting of your Timeshare then e-mail <u>help@time-share-scams.org</u>

The first advice we must give you, is that it is very unlikely you are going to make a profit on your Timeshare. This is not to be negative, but it really will depend on what and where you own. There are Timeshares that hold their value due to location and limited supply. Yet in areas where there is an oversupply of Timeshares, many do sell for a lot less than what was paid.

So, you have to be very realistic when it comes to deciding what price you choose to advertise your Timeshare for, as the price you set will of course dictate how long it is on the market for.

That is why our main recommendation is, always have your Timeshare on a rental listing as well. A high percentage of people wanting to buy a Timeshare will like the opportunity to try and test it before they purchase. It also gives you the chance to build a relationship with your customer.

RENTAL

This is where you can be really proactive in selling your Timeshare. In most cases you will not sell your Timeshare overnight, and if you do not plan to use your ownership while you are waiting to sell, you will still be liable to pay annual fees. This is very important to remember, and can be a major factor in the annoyance of so many Timeshare Owners who are tiresome in their efforts sell.

The annual fees, plus any taxes, have to be paid and you may also still be affiliated to one of the exchange companies. Tie this in with any additional costs you are paying for selling or listing your Timeshare and you can have quite a hefty yearly outlay. You are not using your Timeshare at all and are possibly still paying to go on vacation. No wonder there is such a negative response to Timeshare from unhappy owners.

The world-wide financial crisis has caused a lot of people to panic and rather than spend money, everyone is being more cautious. With most of the general public concerned about job security this will affect people buying Timeshares but WILL lead to an increase in people looking for very good bargains. So don't just plan to sell your Timeshare, list it as a rental as well.

A big mistake here many Timeshare Owners make when listing their ownership for rent is requesting high prices. This, however, may not be the Timeshare Owners fault, as it has been known that huge inflated prices can be quoted by Timeshare companies to persuade you to list your Timeshare rental with them, and pay their high advertisement fee.

"Mr. Johnson your Timeshare regularly rents for $4,000 to $5,000 a week. As we take no commission, it goes straight to you. Our $500 fee is so we make sure your Timeshare reaches the right market."

Like the scams we have mentioned, this can be another way where you end up paying another cost and see no return at all.

Please do not get greedy. Your first target should be to cover all your fees, get the week rented and have a potential buyer using your Timeshare. It is a proven fact that someone would more than likely be interested in buying something, after they have tried and experienced it. And if they don't buy, you will have a happy testimonial from someone who has used your Timeshare that will only build credibility in what your own and are selling.

The main concern here, we repeat, is to get your fees covered and a potential buyer using your Timeshare. So why not rent it at the lowest price you can. As mentioned before, many potential buyers and renters, are looking for a bargain, you are competing in a market that is very competitive, let others list their week for rent in the $2,000 to $3,000 bracket, this will help when you list yours for under $1,000.

And rather than list your Timeshare for sale or rent, along with thousands of others all listed at different prices, we believe by renting your Timeshare you have the opportunity to target a specific market, and this can all be done at virtually no cost at all. YES THAT IS RIGHT. THERE ARE WAYS IN WHICH YOU CAN MARKET YOUR TIMESHARE FOR SALE OR RENT FOR FREE.

Sometimes, your potential buyer could be right on your doorstep. If you own a Timeshare that is on a golf course, why not target golfers? Why not look around at local golf clubs and place an advert on their notice board? If your Timeshare is at a family resort with lots of facilities for children then check the local school notice boards or after school clubs. There is always a free notice board at the local supermarket.

The Internet which can be used as a way to scam Timeshare Owners can also prove beneficial for those who wish to sell or rent their Timeshare and there are many Internet websites and dedicated forums that offer this service for free.

The main reason that we recommend that you target a specific market is that if you go on the Internet and try and rent a Timeshare, for example in Orlando, just by searching some websites that list Timeshare rentals you will get lost amongst all the adverts. We have just done it ourselves, one site had nearly a thousand listed in Orlando alone. Which one do we pick? We want to keep looking in case we miss out on a great deal but after the 7th page of over 100 we got bored.

You have to target the market that will appeal to your Timeshare. It's not rocket science, a golf resort will appeal to golfers, Orlando to families, beach resorts to people who love sun, a ski resort to skiers. This is not to state the obvious, it is because it's important to reinstate that you should really focus on the target market for what you own. What we are saying here is, don't just join the list of Timeshare rental websites that cover the world. A simple ad at the local golf club, or after school club, will make a huge difference. Plus as well you can target close family and friends. You will be surprised how many people that you know who of course trust you that would be happy to snap a bargain of a 2bed apartment that sleeps six for a $1,000 a week, or even better when it is put at under $145 a night.

All it takes is a family looking though the local paper or when picking the children up from the play centre or down at the gym, to see an advert there; Well this can only create more interest for you. Back this up with a webpage or an e-mail with some pictures and you have expanded your target market, and have not had to spend a fortune to do it.

We mentioned earlier that the intention of this book is that Timeshare Scams, which are in operation in the world today, ought to be placed within easy reach of Timeshare Owners who do not have time to investigate them. It is also fair to say, that a high number of Timeshare Owners do not have the time to sell or rent their Timeshare themselves. Also, only a few and if they have the time, know how to set up a web page or e-mail pictures. You should agree though, placing an advert in the local shop, gym sports hall, or golf club is pretty simple, but again it takes time and effort. Hence, you can pay people to do this for you. There are companies that will operate this service, and we would recommend that is the way to go for those that wish too. Again, we hope that with the information provided in this book, we have gone some way to help and warn you of any potential scams. For those who would like further advice and tips please e-mail help@timeshare-scams.org. Upon completion of this book we will dedicate our time to assisting Timeshare Owners wishing to sell or rent their Timeshare.

FINAL THOUGHTS

In simple terms, we could have used just use a few words to write the message of this book.

"Do not pay any money up front on the promise that your Timeshare will be sold or rented for you."

Unfortunately, that message is repeated to thousands of Timeshare Owners daily, but to some the message does not get through. It is hard sometimes to resist the irresistible words of a slick salesman over the phone or the letter that promises you thousands if you just send off your ownership certificate or pay the tax due. Until it happens to you, you just don't know how you would react. Most of us of course, believe that they would not be that stupid, but if you have a few financial problems, maybe have lost money in your 401k, pension or stocks, then with all these money worries that many people have in this world today, it would seem tempting to take a risk when you feel there is a chance that you may make money from your ownership of your Timeshare.

Remember what is being told to you. You are being promised your money back a 100% guarantee, which is backed up with full promises and testimonials from other Timeshare Owners that have used this service.

This book will not stop all the Timeshare Scams that have, and some will still occur all around the world daily, but if one Timeshare Owner after reading this book acts upon the information that we have provided, then it's been worth it. If just one Timeshare Owner manages to use our advice and is able to sell their Timeshare without having to pay out a huge fee, then it has been worth it. If just one Timeshare Owner realizes that it makes sense to look at renting their Timeshare to cover all fees while waiting to sell their Timeshare, then again, it has been worth it.

Please, if you have benefited from the tips and warnings that we have given on Timeshare Scams in operation, then please pass a link to our website www.timeshare-scams.org to other Timeshare Owners, so they can receive updates on any new scams that come into operation.

Timeshares should be considered a product to use and to enjoy future vacations. The percentage of Timeshare Owners that are not happy with their Ownership is minimal when compared with how many are happy.

Timeshare-scams.org warns all Timeshare Owners to be very cautious if they receive an unsolicited approach by a Timeshare company that claim to be able to sell or rent their Timeshare who:

- **Request an up-front fee such as an administration fee.**

- **Offer a guaranteed fully refundable fee if your Timeshare is not sold or rented.**

- **Offer an unrealistic purchase price, often a lot higher than the original price you paid for Your Timeshare**

- **Claim they have a confirmed buyer waiting especially from Asia, the Middle East or Corporate Buyers.**

- **Send a check made out in your name, for a substantial amount of money with the good news that Your Timeshare has sold.**

- **Ask for you to send them your Ownership details.**

As we have stated there are many genuine ways that you can sell or rent your Timeshare but we advise all Timeshare Owners to

- **Always take advice first,**

- **Check Timeshare Forums for comments from genuine Timeshare Owners who have had experiences with the company contacting you,**

- **Do some research on the company making the offer.**

- **To check out the truthfulness of any promises made before making a decision.**

- **And if you do decide to purchase a Timeshare make sure you have a cancellation period which gives you the right to resend with no penalty.**

Timeshare Terminology

A Glossary of Timeshare Terms.

If you are to be personally involved in the process for selling or renting your Timeshare, then it may be worthwhile in you taking a few moments to learn some of the Timeshare terminology. These are words communally used in Timeshare by Owners and Sales staff.

Some of the words that are used in the UK and Europe will be different from words that are frequently used in North America. To save confusion we have included both for your reference.

Accrued Weeks: These are Timeshare Weeks that you have "banked" or "deposited" from the prior year which are available for use in the current calendar year.

Amenities: Features that are on the Timeshare property such as tennis courts, spas, restaurants, 24hr reception, fitness room, golf courses, children's club, laundry facilities, etc. It is known that the more amenities a resort has to offer will only add to the desirability of the property and of course improve your opportunity to sell or rent.

ARDA (The American Resort Development Association): The main trade association in the United States for the timeshare industry. Provides lobbying and other services in support of the industry.

Banking: Depositing a week of timeshare into an exchange company's "bank". If you do not use a week in a particular year, you are generally allowed to bank it and use it at a later time. Normally you can bank a week for up to two years.

Biennial: Use of a Timeshare ownership every other year ('EOY'). Owners are referred to as 'Odd' or 'Even' year owners.

Bonus Time: Use of your resort in addition to your regular allocated time on a space available basis. A Developer Bonus Week (DBW) is available to members who own at participating resort. These bonus weeks are issued directly from the resort, often issued as a signing bonus upon the purchase of a timeshare interval. Sometimes owners can purchase bonus weeks from the resort as unsold developer-owned weeks.

A second type of bonus week is one issued by an exchange company. Owners of high-demand resort weeks receive them as incentives to deposit their timeshare week.

Check-In Date: This simply is the day of week that the Timeshare usage begins; usually Friday, Saturday, or Sunday. The check-in day begins the seven-day Timeshare usage. For example, if the Timeshare week begins on Friday, the week ends on the following Friday. The Timeshare owner (or renter) need not always check in on the specific check-in day; however, late check-in does not extend the Timeshare week beyond the scheduled checkout day. Check-In-Date of course is very important when listing your Timeshare for rent.

Closing Costs: In most cases buying a Timeshare will incur closing costs and these should be listed over and above the purchase fee. These costs will vary depending on whether you pay cash or finance and include deed preparation, recording costs etc. All these costs are associated with the closing process.

Club/Trust Membership: Year-round usage of resort facilities with purchase, on a space available basis. This is the most generally used system of timeshare 'ownership' in the United Kingdom and is growing in popularity everywhere else. Owners belong to a Club; their accommodation unit (and sometimes the leisure facilities) are held by Trustees who license a 'Right-to-Use' to 'Owners'. Sometimes club membership is backed by a deed of ownership, sometimes it is not. (The escritura system in Spain is a deeded system, but deeded timeshare ownership is not legal in the UK and some other countries).

Constitution: This is a collection of documents which establish the relationship between the Timeshare Owner, Developer, Trustee and Management Company. Effectively these are the rules by which the resort is run.

Cooling Off Period: This is a period of time given to a purchaser following the signing of a purchase agreement during which they may cancel their Timeshare purchase without penalty. The length of this time varies from country to country with 14 days in Europe and as low as 5 days in Mexico. In the USA the period varies from state to state.

Deed: A legal document providing title to your property; gives you your ownership rights. Fee Simple.

Deeded Property: True property ownership with deed recorded in the county where the property exists. This type of property has the same rights of ownership accorded to it as other deeded real estate. The owner may sell, rent, bequeath, or give away the property.

Developer's Price: The developer's current or market price for a Timeshare. This is the full retail price and will include the developer's marketing costs. This price will often increase as the Property will be built, often the term Pre-construction will be used.

Escritura: The Spanish term for the deeding and registering of a 'Deed of Title'. Similar to registration of the Land Registry in England and Wales.

Escrow: A special secured account used to hold funds from the buyer and the seller related to closing of purchase and/or sale of a property.

Exchange: The process of trading a Timeshare week at one resort for a Timeshare week at another resort or trading a specific week at the home resort for another week at the same resort. The exchange system allows a Timeshare Owner to trade their week with other Timeshare Owners thereby allowing each owner to travel and vacation throughout the world. Some resorts have internal exchanges with other resorts which are usually owned by the same company.

Fee Simple: The preferred type of real estate ownership. This type of interval ownership is the opposite of Right-to-Use or lease ownership and continues forever. The owner holds a deed in his/her name and the ownership of the property can be bequeathed to heirs.

Fixed Unit: A time period that is fixed for each calendar year, either by date or by calendar weeks; most in numerical sequence 1-52. With a week number, your actual start date may vary slightly from year to year. Unlike a floating unit, a Timeshare Owner who owns a fixed unit at a resort will always vacation in the same physical unit each year he/she vacations at that resort. This type of Ownership is particularly important if you have purchased, for example, an oceanfront property with the ocean at your door step and are not willing to vacation in an ocean-view unit. A fixed unit property assures the Owner that he/she will always have the exact location and the exact unit they have purchased.

Fixed Week: As it says, this is a fixed week of Timeshare Ownership and assures the Owners at the Timeshare Property that they will always have the same week each year, i.e week 24 or week 39 etc. A lot of fixed week ownership comes with fixed unit usage.

Floating: As it says this time your Timeshare Ownership is floating and you use your Ownership at your property at any Time during the floating season you own. In most cases your time period is defined by a season and your week period is not fixed. You reserve your time period within the appropriate season annually. Most resorts have a High, Medium, and Low Season. Please note that Owners of a floating unit at a property might not vacation in the same physical unit each year.

Fractional: Multiple week ownership at the same resort, this is very popular in the high end Timeshare market and is a direct step down of outright Ownership. The property is usually dived up into a share of multiple week Ownership.

Gold Crown: A gold crown resort is RCI's highest rating for a Timeshare resort. This is similar to Interval International's Premier rating.

Guest Certificate: This is a certificate that allows a guest to use the Timeshare instead of the Owner. There is usually a fee involved and is important to note when renting your Timeshare.

Interval International: The second largest exchange company in the world.

Lease/Leasehold: This replaces deeded Ownership as some states and some foreign countries do not allow deeded Ownership of Timeshares.

Alternatively, a lease Ownership or Right-To-Use (RTU) Ownership grants the leasor the right to use the property for a specified period of time; usually from 20 to 99 years.

Lockout/Lock-off Unit: This is a Timeshare unit that has the capability of being divided in two units that can then be used for two separate vacations. Either to make a one week stay at a property becomes two weeks, or converts the One week Timeshare by lockout and then use the two weeks for exchange. Many Timeshare Owners even rent one unit to cover any annual fees due and use the other for vacations. Please note normally you will incur a lock-off fee.

Maintenance Fee: Maintenance fees are established and collected by the Home Owners Association or Resort Management Company to maintain the property, pay insurance, utilities, refurbishing and taxes. These fees vary from resort to resort and with the type and size of the unit purchased. The cost of resort operation is spread among Owners. This fee must also build up reserves to pay for non-recurring costs like furniture, appliances etc. that need periodic replacement and other capital costs as normal physical deterioration occurs.

Management Company: The Company contracted, usually by the Owners Club/Home Owners Association, to carry out all the day-to-day management of the resort. Very often owned or controlled by the developer.

Management Fees: The fees usually paid annually, by each Owner or points club member to cover the costs of running the resort on a day-to-day basis.

Maximum Occupancy: The maximum number of persons a Timeshare unit will accommodate; usually from 2 to 10 persons. Maximum occupancy is typically expressed in conjunction with "private occupancy" referring to the number of persons the unit will sleep privately and the number of bedrooms within the unit. Configurations of units vary from resort to resort.

Points: Programs offered to Timeshare Owners by resorts which allow the Owners choice and control over when and where they vacation or for how long or short they stay. Points value can vary by size, season, resort location, length of stay and can offer a Timeshare Owner more flexibility

Points Clubs: A Timeshare system where 'Owners' hold points which entitle them to use a period (varying from a few days to a few weeks) every year from a choice of resorts. Sometimes points are backed by an actual deed, sometimes they are not.

Property Bonds: A system similar to Points clubs for owning shares or bonds in a company owning properties.

RCI: Resorts Condominiums International the largest exchange company in the world.

RDO Resort Development Organization (Formally known as Organization for Timeshare in Europe): The European equivalent of ARDA, but more consumers oriented.

Right To Use (RTU): Occupancy rights for a specified number of years, with no Ownership interest in the property. Some states and some foreign countries do not allow deeded Ownership of Timeshares. Alternatively, a lease Ownership or Right-To-Use Ownership grants the lesser the right to use the property for a specified period of time; usually from 20 to 99 years. The resort developer or Management Company holds Ownership of the physical property. However, during the right-to-use period, the owner may rent, transfer, or bequeath the remaining years of their right-to-use property.

Season: These are periods of Time throughout the year which the Timeshare Owner will own and can use at their property of Ownership or exchange for the same season or of less value. RCI exchange seasons are Red (high) White (mid) and Blue (low) Interval International Seasons of exchange are Red (high) Yellow (mid) and Green (low).

Trustees: A bank, trust company or a group of individuals who hold Timeshare accommodation (and sometimes leisure facilities) 'in trust' on behalf of the Owners and grant Owners a 'right –to-use' through a license ('Ownership Certificate'). Trustees provide security for owners in the event that a developer fails financially. Some trustees may have added responsibilities such as ensuring the continuity of the Owners Club.

Trading Power: A word often used within Timeshare. To keep it simple, supply and demand dictates how this works for exchange and Timeshare Owners can greatly improve their chances of better exchanges by owning a Timeshare high demand weeks or at properties with less supply.

Unit Size: Very simply this means what it says Unit Size. This will mean a studio unit, efficiency unit or size by number of bedrooms. Hotel units, studio units, and efficiency units typically are a single room with sleeping accommodations and perhaps a small built in kitchen and sleep from two to four persons. One, two or three or more bedroom units are usually condominium style accommodations and feature a partial or full kitchen and other living areas.

Vacation Ownership: This is another term for Timeshare. In Europe can be referred to as Holiday Ownership.

Made in the USA